Violent Feelings

Pete Sanders

Aladdin / Watts
London • Sydney

© Aladdin Books Ltd 2004

Designed and produced by
Aladdin Books Ltd
28 Percy Street
London W1T 2BZ

New edition
first published in
Great Britain in 2004 by
Franklin Watts
96 Leonard Street
London EC2A 4XD

ISBN 0 7496 5402 3

Original edition published as
What Do You Know About –
Feeling Violent

Editor
Katie Harker

Designer
Flick, Book Design & Graphics
Simon Morse

Illustrator
Mike Lacey

Picture Research
Brian Hunter Smart

CONTENTS

How to use this book

The books in this series deal with issues that
may affect the lives of many young people.

- Each book can be read by a young person
  alone, or together with an adult.

- Issues raised in the storyline are further
  discussed in accompanying text.

- A list of practical ideas is given in the 'What
  can we do?' section at the end of the book.

- Organisations and helplines are listed for
  additional information and support.

INTRODUCTION

It was horrible. One minute they were talking rationally and then, all of a sudden, they were kicking and screaming at each other. I didn't know how to stop them.

We are all affected by acts of violence at some time in our lives. You may have seen violence on TV, watched others fighting, or you may even have been involved in a violent incident yourself. Most people have also felt violent at some time or other. It is hard to deal with these feelings when they happen. Sadly, violence has now become a regular part of many people's lives.

This book will help you to find out more about the causes and effects of violence. Each chapter introduces a different aspect of the subject, illustrated by a continuing storyline. The characters in the story are involved in situations which affect many people in their everyday lives. After each episode, we stop and consider the issues raised, and open out the discussion. By the end of the book, you will understand more about why violence happens, know about different ways of dealing with violent feelings and be able to make your own choices and decisions about the place that violence has in your own life.

WHAT IS VIOLENCE?

" There's a gang at school who have a reputation for bullying. They like to intimidate people. If you want to get along, it's best to just stay out of their way. "

Watching the news on TV, or reading a newspaper recently, you have probably seen reports of violence. Violence means any act of force which harms people or property.

If you fight, or threaten to hit someone, you are behaving violently. Bullies at school often use violence to try to get others to act in the way they want, or to hand over money or property. People who behave like this have planned to be violent. Their actions do not happen on the spur of the moment, but have been thought through beforehand. Sometimes a bully may become violent because they are being bullied themselves, or because they are experiencing violence at home.

Violence can also flare up suddenly. If you have ever lost your temper, you know that this can happen very quickly. Some people have a very bad temper, which they find difficult to control. When people like that become angry, they can be frightening, and may hurt others without meaning to.

Sometimes bullies get their way by threatening to use violence. By exerting power in this way, bullies may not actually use physical violence, but their threats can be just as damaging to a victim.

4

Emily and her friend Lauren were discussing their homework. They had to write about a news story.

I've done mine about the factory fire. Five people were killed.

I chose that case about the two kids who beat up an old lady. One of them was only nine.

The whole class knew about Emily's news story. One of the boys lived in the neighbourhood.

Why do you think those children would do something like this?

My dad says it's the parents' fault, and they should be locked away, too.

At playtime, Emily and Lauren couldn't stop thinking about the case.

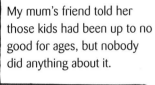

My mum's friend told her those kids had been up to no good for ages, but nobody did anything about it.

GIRL, 10, BOY, 9 QUESTIONED ABOUT BRUTAL BEATING

Emily had seen David with new toys which she knew he couldn't afford.

I'd tell on him if I could prove it.

David's always bunking off school, and getting into fights. Do you think he might end up like those other two?

It wouldn't surprise me. I know for a fact he damages property.

The girls watched David and his friend bullying another boy. David was always in trouble for fighting.

I don't think we should say anything. I'm scared of him. He's got an awful temper.

Do you think Emily and Lauren should tell on David?

5

David is an example of someone who uses violence to get his own way. His reputation for having a fierce temper makes others afraid to do anything about his bullying. If you, or someone you know, is being threatened, talk to a friend, a teacher, your parents or someone you trust. It can be difficult to confront a bully on your own, but involving other people will help you to stand up to the violence.

They are many kinds of crime

A crime is any action which is forbidden by law. Crimes range from murder and theft to dropping litter and causing a nuisance by being noisy. Most acts of violence are also crimes.

- Hitting someone is a crime called 'assault'.

- Laws are made by the government to protect people and property. The police ensure that laws are obeyed, and arrest people who break them.

- Today, more and more criminals use violence when they commit crimes.

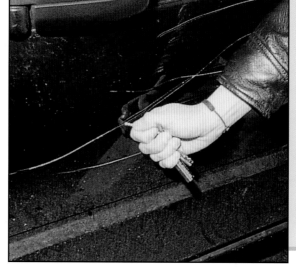

Vandalism is a kind of violence. It is any action which deliberately damages property. Some acts of vandalism are done to try to upset a particular person. Often, though, people damage property because they are jealous they don't own it themselves. Or they may perform acts of vandalism out of boredom. Sometimes, vandals say they are just fooling around. If accused of vandalism, David might try to excuse himself in this way.

WHY DO PEOPLE USE VIOLENCE?

> 66 We were just fooling around. There's nothing to do in the evenings around here. It was just a bit of fun – we didn't think it would hurt anyone. 99

There are many different reasons why people act violently. Some young people use violence when they want to look big or to impress others. Others behave violently because they bear a grudge, or because they are angry or frustrated.

Some people think they can use violence to scare people into doing what they want. Others may join in to be part of a gang, or because they are copying someone they look up to.

Some parents behave violently towards children, even very young babies, when they are feeling impatient or under great stress. Children who have been treated violently from an early age may believe that violence is perfectly natural. They may go on to use violence themselves, because they do not know another way to express their feelings, and have never learned to communicate in other ways.

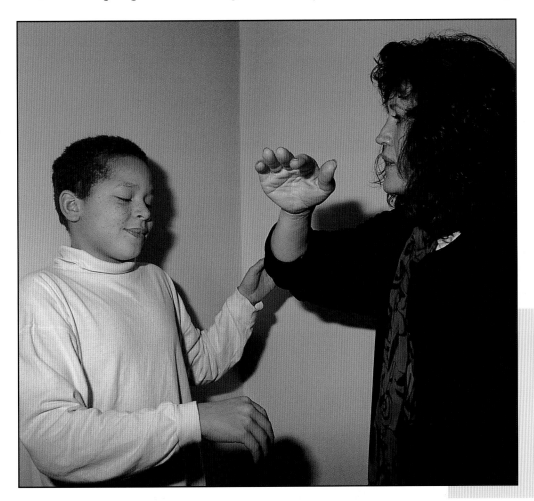

Some adults use their greater size and strength to force children to do what they want to do.

The next day...

... David's brother, Tom, was the leader of a gang. The gang was always in trouble, but David had never been involved with them before.

The gang explained the plan to David.

David kept watch as the gang stole Michael's bike.

Michael was punched and left on the pavement.

Tom was pleased with David.

Why do you think David went along with the gang?

> Hey, leave me alone.
> You're not taking my bike!

People who intend to be violent often choose an 'easy target' as their victim, because they know that they are more likely to get away with their actions.

Tom and his gang knew that Michael would be alone. Michael was greatly outnumbered and there was no one there to defend him when Tom threatened him with a knife.

> Then I'll have a knife, too.

Some people enjoy the feeling of trying to get away with something they should not be doing.

Like David, it may be that they start off by doing little things they know are wrong. If they don't get caught, they may then be tempted to try even more daring things. But sooner or later they'll realise they won't be able to get away with it.

Some people get into trouble because they are bored.

They may try to excuse some kinds of violence, such as vandalism, by saying that there is nothing else for them to do. This is particularly a problem amongst young people, who are not old enough to work and who may not be engaged in activities that fill their hours. Many adults want more money to be spent on providing activities and youth clubs that keep young people entertained and away from a life of crime.

GANGS

When you're in town on a Saturday night you can spot the rival gangs a mile off. They're always looking for trouble. Most weekends there's some fight or other.

Gangs go around together because it can be fun to be part of a group. Sometimes, though, gang members will dare each other, and this can lead to trouble.

Some gangs attract people who want to appear tough. Gang members may try to prove how tough they are by challenging other gangs to a fight. 'Gang warfare' of this kind is used to assert superiority. Some gangs have very strict rules. They may decide that members of a rival gang are not allowed to walk down a certain street, or play in a particular area. If others break these 'rules', there may be a fight. Gangs thrive on intimidation and like to have a bad reputation.

The way that many gang activities are conducted, encourage young people to view criminal activities, such as vandalism or drug abuse, as a form of fun. People who go around in gangs often find it hard to refuse to join in with the others. The pressure to go along with what is happening can be very strong. Going against the crowd often takes great courage.

When you are part of a gang, it is easy to forget that you have a right to your own opinion.

> I don't like this at all. They say Sam even nicks cars. Be careful.

When situations get out of control, it can be difficult to remember that other people are individuals, with feelings just as important as your own. You can begin to see others as your 'enemy', without thinking about their reasons for disagreeing with you. This is particularly true if you are part of a gang. Tom and Sam had forgotten that disputes have more than one side to the story.

> He likes to think he's tough. We'll see about that. You leave this to me.

It is not a good idea to take the law into your own hands. You can't always predict what will happen and could find yourself in a lot of trouble. If Michael had talked to an adult he trusted, or had gone to the police, the outcome would have been very different.

> I hear your brother likes picking on little kids. You tell him from me – there's going to be trouble.

Revenge can often lead to violence. Sometimes people are violent because they want to get their own back on others. Personal disputes can also get out of control if others are encouraged to join in. Instead of solving anything, fighting made Michael and Sam's situation worse. The boys are now even less likely to see each other's point of view.

LIVING WITH VIOLENCE

> **Dad's been hitting Mum for a few years now. It mostly happens when he's been drinking. We try to stop him, but he lashes out at us as well. I don't know what to do.**

In some families there are adults who are violent with each other, and with their children. These people often get away with violence because other members of the family are afraid to tell anyone about it.

The reasons for the violence are not always obvious. Although family members are the ones to suffer, the anger may be caused by something outside the family. People who cannot get a job, or who worry about not having enough money to get by, may become angry and hurt those closest to them. People who are very unhappy with their lives may use violence to take out their feelings on others.

A person who is being violent needs help. Some people who are violent refuse to admit they have a problem, or do not know how to get help. Other members of the family may also try to pretend that nothing's wrong. If there is violence within your family, it is not your fault. Always try to talk to someone you can trust about the situation.

Some people become violent when they have been drinking alcohol.

A week later...

... the gang leaders had been recognised.
Tom and Sam were both cautioned by the police.

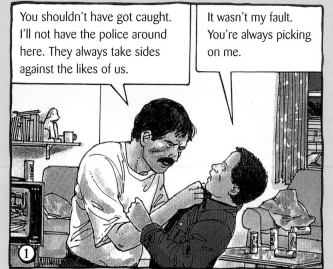

Sam's father did not like the police being involved. He had been drinking and became angry.

Sam hated his parents arguing. He and his friend Scott went to find their friend Adam.

Adam explained his plan to the others.

Despite what everyone thought,
Sam had never stolen a car before.

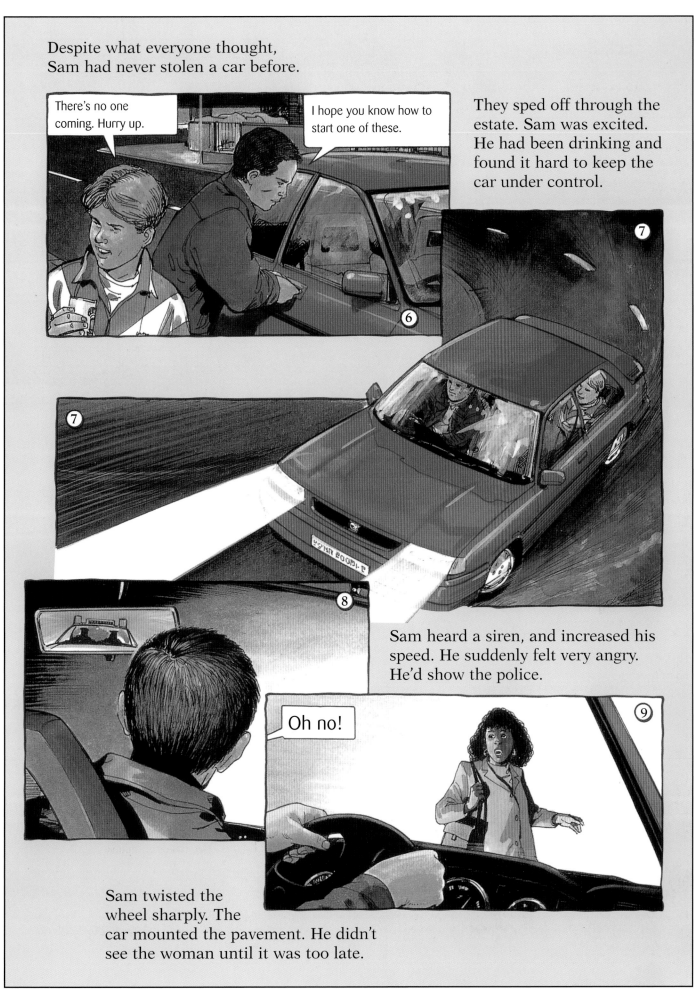

They sped off through the estate. Sam was excited. He had been drinking and found it hard to keep the car under control.

Sam heard a siren, and increased his speed. He suddenly felt very angry. He'd show the police.

Sam twisted the wheel sharply. The car mounted the pavement. He didn't see the woman until it was too late.

> You shouldn't have got caught. I'll not have the police round here.

Alcohol alters the way we think and feel.

Many people enjoy a drink. However, like Sam's father, some people become aggressive when they have been drinking. People who are drunk are not fully in control of their actions, but they may not be aware that alcohol is affecting them in this way. This is why there are strict laws about not driving after drinking alcohol. Some people, like Sam, become reckless when they drink, and may do something they wouldn't do if they were sober.

Alcohol can be a habit

Drinking alcohol can become a habit – called an 'addiction'.

- Some people come to rely on alcohol and believe they cannot do without it.

- At its worst, this kind of addiction can rule their lives.

- An emotional dependence on alcohol often means that a person is, or will become, physically addicted as well.

> I've had enough of this. I'm going out.

If someone in a family is addicted to alcohol, both family and friends will be affected, too.

Sam went out because his father had been drinking and had become violent. Sadly, people who are trying to escape violent situations at home often find themselves getting into other kinds of trouble.

IS THERE MORE VIOLENCE TODAY?

> " Sometimes, the violence that's portrayed in films is meant to be funny. It's strange to be laughing at something you would normally be shocked to see in real life. "

There seem to be more and more reports of crime and violence today, particularly amongst young people. No one knows why this is. It may be that more violence and crime are reported, or that with increased media coverage, we hear more about violence now than we used to.

Television itself has also been blamed for the increase in crime and violence. It has been suggested that some programmes and films make violence seem more acceptable. Advertisers have also been blamed for showing a glamorous world which many people want, but cannot afford. Some people think it is the fault of adults for being less strict than they used to be, and allowing children to get away with too much. They believe that adults need to help children to understand that violence and crime are not acceptable behaviour.

Some adults believe that the world was a safer place in the old days and that children could play safely without supervision. Not everyone agrees with this idea.

After the crash...

... Adam had run away before the police arrived.
Sam was arrested. The woman had been badly injured.

Sam's solicitor explained the situation to him.

But Sam suddenly had an idea how he could get his own back on Tom.

You certainly seem to have got a reputation for causing trouble.

Sam has a reputation for always being in trouble.

Some people think it is important to appear tough all the time. They want to impress, or be accepted by, others. This can lead to them being blamed for something they did not do. As Sam has found out, once people have formed an opinion about you, it can be very difficult to prove them wrong.

It wasn't my idea in the first place. I always get blamed for everything. It was the same at school.

People sometimes use violence to hide how they are really feeling.

They may be afraid of someone finding out they are not good at something. We already know that Sam can't read properly. People like him may become angry and refuse to do something, hoping that others will notice only their anger. They may throw a temper tantrum to get out of having to do something they cannot do well.

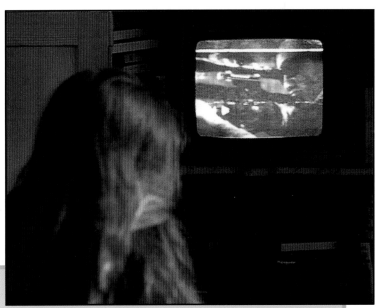

Some adults think that being exposed to violence can make people act violently.

There is more violence on television, in films and in newspapers than there used to be. Some people think this makes us accept violence more easily. Other disagree. It is important to remember that what you watch in films is often make-believe. It may look exciting, but trying to copy what you see on screen could lead to someone being hurt for real.

FEELING ANGRY

" I couldn't believe that he could accuse me
like that. I felt so angry. I went really flushed
and was shaking. If I hadn't walked away
I'm sure I would have hit him. "

Everyone feels angry from time to time. Anger is a completely normal human emotion. But when anger gets out of control it can lead to violence. It is sometimes very difficult to hold your temper. The feelings you have are strong, and it may seem impossible not to act on them.

There is nothing wrong with feeling angry, but it is important to learn to control your temper. If you are having an argument with someone, it may be frustrating if you are not given the chance to answer back, or express your own point of view. You may feel very annoyed, and perhaps be tempted to take it out on someone else.

Anger can flare up quickly, but it often goes away just as fast. Leaving a situation for a few minutes can help to calm angry feelings. You will then be able to judge the situation more clearly. Even if you are in the right, it is sometimes best to wait before reacting too quickly. If you do something in anger, you may regret it later.

Sometimes when we are angry, we take our feelings out on people who may not be to blame.

Two days later...

... Emily and Lauren had heard about Tom's arrest. He had not had an alibi for the night of the crash.

The two girls tried to reason with David. But David wouldn't listen.

David started to fight with Lauren.

Emily suddenly felt very angry, and began to hit David.

Do you think Emily was right to hit David?

21

Where will that get you?
You'd just be in trouble too.

As Emily, David and Lauren are learning, fighting usually causes more problems than it solves. Using physical violence will not help you to sort out a difficulty. In the heat of the moment it can also be easy to hurt somebody badly, without meaning to do so. It can be difficult to stand back. But learning to do this can help to prevent some violent situations. Simple relaxation techniques, such as deep breathing, can help to calm down angry feelings. Walking away for a few minutes can also relieve your anger.

Discussions are useful

If you disagree with someone, you should say what you think calmly, and give reasons.

- One person shouting at another is rarely helpful. Be prepared to really listen to what the other person is saying.

- Recognising when someone may be angry, and trying not to provoke them further, can help to stop some situations from becoming violent.

It's understandable. We should talk to him. He really believes Tom didn't do it.

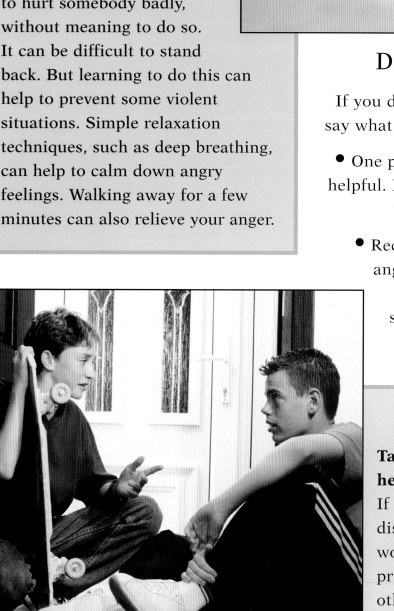

Talking about your feelings can help to sort out problems. If you bottle things up and don't discuss them, you will probably feel worse. A problem shared is often a problem halved – remember that other people may have ideas about how to handle a situation.

TAKING RESPONSIBILITY

> *I didn't like what was going on and I had to speak out. I was worried about how the others would react, but at the end of the day I was true to myself, and that's what matters.*

You may have heard friends say that someone else made them do something they are in trouble for. You may even have used this excuse yourself, to avoid taking the blame for something. As we grow older, most of us realise that we must be responsible for what we say and do.

Denying that an event ever occurred or blaming others instead of taking responsibility are all common tactics that people use to avoid difficult situations. But we learn that blaming others for our behaviour is not right. It is likely that there have been times in your life when you went along with what others were doing, even though you didn't want to. It can be difficult to refuse to do something if everyone else is joining in. Saying no to something you know is wrong is hard, especially if you are being threatened, or think you may lose a friendship. Most people are scared of being rejected. But if you don't say no, you may end up in trouble and not respecting yourself.

Often you will gain respect by speaking your mind, and not just going along with the gang. You may even find that others feel the way you do, but were afraid to speak up.

Mrs Anderson took them inside and asked what had happened. Emily blamed David.

Emily thought a lot about what Mrs Anderson had said about different kinds of violence.

Mrs Anderson talked to them for a while, and tried to help them see each other's point of view.

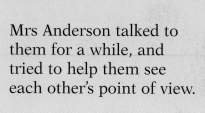

It sounds like you all need to learn how to control your tempers.

It is helpful to try to understand how other people are feeling.

Mrs Anderson helped Emily, Lauren and David to realise that we don't all see situations in the same way all the time. If you want to have respect from other people, you must remember that they want to be respected too. This means that you must also be prepared to listen to their side of the story.

There are times when we all have to own up to being wrong.

This can be very difficult. But if you continue to defend your actions, as David and Emily did at first, the situation will not improve. It may be hard to take the blame, but by doing so you will prevent things from getting out of hand later on.

I can't believe I hit David. That's not like me.

Some feelings are more difficult to talk about.

It can often be hard to understand why we are feeling the way we are at a particular moment. Sometimes feelings can take us by surprise. The world affects us all in different ways. Don't be afraid to express how you are feeling.

HOW CAN WE STOP VIOLENCE?

" If the bullies at school had a taste of their
own medicine, I'm sure they'd soon stop
what they were doing. "

Violence is a continuing problem but there are lots of different ideas about how it can be prevented. Having read this book, you may now have ideas of your own.

Some people think that violence would be reduced if there were even tougher punishments for violent crimes. This might make people think twice about being violent in the first place, or be deterred from reoffending.

It is also thought that those who commit acts of violence need to appreciate the effect that their actions have on other people. Perhaps violent people would change the way they behave if they had a better understanding of the suffering they cause. Some adults believe that young people need to be taught about the problem of violence from an early age, so that children learn not to accept violence as a natural way of behaving.

If you are feeling angry, it can sometimes be helpful to channel your energy into sport. If you're feeling frustrated, you can always take your aggression out on the ball!

26

Some months later...

... Sam had finally admitted in court that Tom was not involved. Tom had been released.

> Well I guess Sam will be out of trouble for a while.

> I'm glad they found out the truth about Tom.

> It's David I feel sorry for. He was so much better when Tom wasn't around.

> He's hanging out with other people now. I think he'll be ok.

When Emily's mum returned from shopping, Lauren told her what they had been talking about.

> Prison's too good for people like Sam. They're too soft on them in there.

> I agree with Lauren. I think Sam should be made to help out other people, not just put in prison.

Mrs Anderson told the class they could have a short discussion about the case.

> How are you David? I hear you're using up your energy playing sport now.

Now the case was in the news again, everyone was talking about it.

> I want everyone to be quiet.

> I think it's great. It must have been fun driving that car.

> Yes, but that woman still can't walk properly.

> Yes. I play football twice a week now. I go to a club.

> Just talking about things can help, for a start.

The class have begun to come up with their own ideas about how violence can be stopped. Schools increasingly teach anger management skills and encourage pupils to look at ways that violence can be prevented. The local police also provide schools with information about crime and violence and give young people advice about how to stay out of trouble.

> Maybe a job will keep him out of trouble when he gets out.

Not everyone agrees that punishment alone changes the way that people behave. Emily now understands that learning a job in prison might help Sam when he is released. Sam got into trouble partly because he was bored and unhappy. Often, people like Sam need help to change the circumstances that led to their turning to crime and violence. Making changes for the better can help criminals to resist the temptation to repeat their actions.

How to punish violence

Punishment is used to make a person think more carefully about their future actions.

- Some people think that the threat of punishment helps a child to avoid trouble.

- Others think that children should learn by their mistakes and avoid trouble in future because they know it is wrong.

WHAT CAN WE DO?

> *I used to blame myself for the hard time I was getting at school. Somehow I thought I deserved the bullying. But then I told my parents what was going on – I wish I'd told them a long time ago!*

Having read this book, you will understand more about the causes of violence and the effects that violence can have on people's lives.

By now you will probably have your own thoughts about how you can help to prevent violence. It is important to judge each situation carefully. Avoiding circumstances when violence might happen can often prevent a problem before it begins. You have also learned a lot about different ways to handle violent feelings. If you are feeling angry or frustrated, talking about it with someone you can trust, and not acting on the spur of the moment, will help. You may want to leave the situation for a while, put your energy into playing sport or go for a run until you have calmed down. It's also never too late to seek help if you, or a friend, are experiencing problems to do with crime or violence.

Violence affects everyone – not just the people who are being violent and their victims. Those who know about it, or who watch it happen, are affected, too.

Adults and children who have read this book together may find it helpful to share their thoughts and ideas about the issues raised. Sometimes adults need help with problems involving crime and violence, too. Many of the organisations listed below provide information, advice and support for both adults and children – those who use violence and those who have been treated violently. Nobody should have to put up with violence. Together we can help to stop it.

National Children's Bureau
8 Wakley Street
London
EC1V 7QE
Tel: 020 7843 6000
Email: membership@ncb.org.uk
Website: www.ncb.org.uk

Childline
45 Folgate Street
London E1 6GL
Tel: 020 7650 3200
24-hour helpline:
0800 11 11
Textphone: 0800 400 222
Website: www.childline.org.uk

The Samaritans
The Upper Mill
Kingston Road
Ewell
Surrey KT17 2AF
Tel: 020 8394 8300
24-hour helpline:
0845 7 90 90 90
Email: admin@samaritans.org
Website: www.samaritans.org.uk

Children's Legal Centre
The Children's Legal Centre
University of Essex
Wivenhoe Park
Colchester CO4 3SQ
Advice line: 01206 873820
Email: clc@essex.ac.uk
Website: www.childrenslegalcentre.com

National Society for the Prevention of Cruelty to Children (NSPCC)
Weston House
42 Curtain Road
London
EC2A 3NH
Tel: 020 7825 2500
24-hour helpline:
0808 800 5000
Email: help@nspcc.org.uk
Website: www.nspcc.org.uk

Alcohol Concern
Waterbridge House
32-36 Loman Street
London SE1 0EE
Tel: 020 7928 7377
Email: contact@alcoholconcern.org.uk
Website: www.alcoholconcern.org.uk

National Association for the Care & Resettlement of Offenders (NACRO)
169 Clapham Road
London
SW9 0PU
Tel 020 7582 6500
Email: communications@nacro.org.uk
Website: www.nacro.org.uk

Child Abuse Prevention Service, Australia (CAPS)
13 Norton Street
Ashfield
New South Wales 2131
Australia
Tel: (02) 9716 8000
Email: mail@childabuseprevention.com.au
Website: www.childabuseprevention.com.au

Children's Protection Society, Australia (CPS)
70 Altona Street
Heidelberg
West Victoria 3081
Australia
Tel: (03) 9458 3566
Email: cps@cps.org.au
Website: www.cps.org.au

INDEX